A DAY IN THE LIFE OF A
Forest Ranger

by David Paige

photography by Michael Mauney

Troll Associates

Library of Congress Catalog Card Number: 78-68809
ISBN 0-89375-227-4   ISBN 0-89375-231-2 Paper Edition

The author and publisher wish to thank the U.S. Forest Service, U.S. Department of Agriculture, for their
generous assistance and cooperation, especially the Regional Forester Office, Milwaukee, Wisconsin; the Forest
Supervisor, Nicolet National Forest, Rhinelander, Wisconsin; and the District Ranger Office, Florence,
Wisconsin.
Photograph credits: pp. 8, 28 — Forest Service, U.S.D.A.; pp. 9, 18, 20 — Lynn Rogers; pp. 16, 30 — Richard
Whittingham.

Lee Schaar looks after a lot of territory. As a district ranger for the U.S. Forest Service, he takes care of a larger area than most big cities cover. But it's all forest land, and the only people who make their homes here are Lee and his family.

There are more than 800 district rangers in charge of the U.S. national forests. Part of their work is done from behind a desk. They plan tree removal and wildlife projects. They keep records and write reports. They answer letters and telephone calls. Ranger Schaar starts a lot of his days getting some paperwork out of the way.

But most of his work is outdoors. And by nine a.m., that is usually where you will find him. This morning, two canoeists have paddled in behind the ranger station to ask the best routes between lakes in the district. Lee knows every stream and trail in his territory.

Before he begins his daily rounds, Lee takes his daughters to see the ducklings. A week ago, a camper brought in a baby duck. She thought it had been abandoned by its mother. But really the duckling had gotten lost, so Lee returned it to its family. Now he wants to make sure no more have wandered off.

Every day Lee has certain places he visits. To get where he has to go today, he will go by boat around the lake, by jeep along the roads, and by foot when the roads become narrow forest paths. He will be gone all day today. His daughters help him load his gear.

The ranger's territory is true wilderness. But he is far from alone in it. Besides people who camp, hike, hunt and fish, there are hundreds and hundreds of animals. There are fish and birds, chipmunks, beavers, and bears. There are deer, too — about two thousand of them in Lee's district.

Some animals, like bears and wolves, can be dangerous. But most forest animals are not dangerous. A few, like the raccoon, seem too busy to even bother with outsiders. Lee knows the habits and needs of all the animals in his district. Looking after their welfare is part of his job.

Lee's first stop is the Youth Conservation Corps camp. The YCC is a program sponsored by the U. S. Forest Service for 15- to 18-year-olds. They work and study in the field with rangers and foresters. They live at the camp for weeks at a time.

As the YCC kids put the finishing touches on a dock they are building, Ranger Schaar supervises their work. Besides dock building, they have also chopped out trails, cleared areas for recreation and camping, pruned trees, and cleaned up the clutter from the forest floor. In addition, they have worked on various wildlife projects — such as installing feed boxes for birds.

The ranger leaves the YCC camp and gets back in his boat. He wants to check the shoreline for erosion, and for trees that have fallen or are about to fall. Fallen trees can be hazardous to boat traffic and to people who use the lakeshore areas. But someone is trying to get his attention.

"A bear!" the man tells him. "We came back to our camp and a bear was raiding the garbage. I guess we surprised him. When he reared up and growled, he scared us so much that Mark fell and cut his arm. We were afraid he was going to attack us, but he ran off in that direction."

The ranger bandages Mark's arm. "Stop at the clinic in town," he tells Mark's father. "That cut may need a few stitches." He also asks them to break camp. "There aren't many bears here usually, but sometimes they get to liking campers' garbage better than what they normally eat. This one may be back to finish his lunch."

As the campers pack up, Lee radios the ranger station. "There's a bear hanging around a campsite here. Send one of the foresters right away." Then Lee radios the state's Department of Natural Resources. He tells them he'll need a couple of men and a truck to move the bear out to the backlands.

Rangers often fly from place to place in the wilderness. Sometimes flying is the only way to get to a remote area of the forest. Other times, it is simply the quickest. A pontoon plane brings a forester to help Ranger Schaar capture the bear.

There are two ways to capture a bear. One is to trap it in a cage, move the cage to a distant part of the forest, and open the cage. The second way is to shoot the animal with a tranquilizing gun. The gun fires a dart filled with a drug to knock the bear unconscious. The two men have the tranquilizing gun ready. They wait for the bear to come back.

"There he is," says Ranger Schaar, as a full-grown black bear comes into view. Lee has seen more frightening bears in other forests. When he was in Montana — training to become a ranger — Lee saw a grizzly bear that was much bigger, and much more dangerous.

But a huge black bear can be dangerous, too. So Lee waits quietly and watches closely as the bear approaches. The forester takes careful aim, and fires. The tranquilizing dart hits right on the mark.

Within seconds the tranquilizer takes effect. The bear will be unconscious for about ten minutes. When the two men from the Department of Natural Resources arrive, they will load the bear into a cage in the back of their truck. Then they will relocate the animal in a remote area of the forest.

After the bear is taken care of, the ranger has to take care of the "bear bait" — the mess of garbage. He picks it all up, even the smallest scraps. Then he takes the bag to the garbage depot along the main road. A forester will be along later to pick it up.

The excitement of the morning is over. Lee sits
down by a bubbling stream to have a quiet lunch.
The lush, green forest is all around him. He loves
the woods. He always has. That's why he studied
forestry in college. After he graduated, he worked
his way up as a forester before he was appointed
ranger.

Improving the forest is an important part of a ranger's job. Sometimes that means removing trees that are dead or dying, or ones that grow too close together. Whenever Lee decides a tree must be removed, he marks it with a spray of paint. Later, a logger will cut it down.

Loggers work in the woods every day. Sometimes they just weed out certain trees. Other times they clear entire areas. These tree trunks will be taken to a mill where they will be made into paper. The logger can only do his work with the permission of the ranger.

The protection of the forest and the wildlife in it is the ranger's main concern. The only logging operations that can be carried out are those that will not harm either the forest or the animals in it. Loggers, too, have a respect for the wilderness. That's why this logger is telling Lee about someone nearby who is not being careful about his campfire.

Lee takes a look for himself. The campfire is not safe. It is too close to an area of dry leaves and branches. Now, the fire is simple to put out. He shovels dirt on it. But if it had spread — and it could have, with nothing more than a gust of wind — it might have turned into a full-fledged forest fire.

A ranger's firefighting equipment consists of a fireproof jacket, hard hat, water tanks and hose gun, and an asbestos bag that he can roll up in if he can't escape the fire. During his years as a forester and a ranger, Lee has fought against some tremendous forest fires.

When a large forest fire does rage out of control, rangers and foresters are brought in from all over the country to help fight it. At one of the largest fires that Lee Schaar fought, he was part of a team of more than 10,000 persons who fought the fire. A big fire may burn for weeks before it is finally brought under control.

It has been a full day for Ranger Schaar. Most work days are over when he gets home, around five o'clock. But today isn't one of those days. In fact, he only has time to say hello to his family and pick up his dinner and bedroll. Tonight he will sleep in the forest.

Some parts of the forest are very remote. There are no paths or roads that lead into them. The edge of one of these areas is where the bear was released earlier in the day. These places are just as much a part of the ranger's responsibility as those where people camp.

Lee wants to start his field work tomorrow at daybreak. The best way to do that is to go out tonight and camp there. That way, he can put in a full day's work before the pontoon plane comes to take him back tomorrow night.

A sleeping bag might not be as comfortable as a bed. But it is beautiful and quiet in the forest. The only sounds come from the leaves that whisper in the wind, and from the animals that make their homes here. Soon darkness will fall silently on the forest, marking the end of another day in the life of a forest ranger.